NIGHT SKY

and Other
Amazing Sights in Space

Comets

Nick Hunter

Heinemann
LIBRARY
Chicago, Illinois

Edited by Rebecca Rissman, Daniel Nunn,
and Sian Smith
Designed by Joanna Hinton-Malivoire and Marcus Bell
Picture research by Mica Brancic
Production by Sophia Argyris
Originated by Capstone Global Library Ltd
Printed and bound in China by South China Printing
Company Ltd

17 16 15 14 13
10 9 8 7 6 5 4 3 2 1

Library of Congress Cataloging-in-Publication Data
Hunter, Nick.
Comets / Nick Hunter.—1st ed.
       p. cm.—(The night sky: and other amazing sights)
Includes bibliographical references and index.
ISBN 978-1-4329-7514-2 (hb)
ISBN 978-1-4329-7519-7 (pb)

1. Comets—Juvenile literature. I. Title.
  QB721.5.H86 2014
  523.6—dc23   2012043045

Acknowledgments
The author and publisher are grateful to the following
for permission to reproduce copyright material: Alamy
pp.17 (© B.A.E. Inc.), 27 (© Mark Hamilton); Capstone
Publishers pp.28, 29 (© Karon Dubke); Corbis p.25 (©
Roger Ressmeyer); Gemini Observatory p.20; Getty
Images p.24 (Fotosearch); NASA pp.22, 10 (University
of Maryland/JPL-Caltech), 14 (JPL-Caltech/UCLA), 21
(Jet Propulsion Laboratory Collection), 23 (JPL-Caltech/
UMD); Robert Harding p.7 (Walter Rawlings); Science
Photo Library pp.8 (Walter Pacholka, Astropics), 9
(Richard Kail), 11 (European Southern Observatory),
12 (Detlev Van Ravenswaay), 13 (Julian Baum), 15
(Alex Cherney, Terrastro.com), 16 (Jerry Lodriguss),
18 (NASA/ESA/STSCI/H. Hammel, MIT), 26 (Gordon
Garradd); Shutterstock pp.4 (© pixelparticle), 5 (©
Primoz Cigler), 19 (© Molodec); TopFoto p.6 (World
History Archive).

Cover illustration of a comet in space reproduced with
permission of Shutterstock (© xjbxjhxm123).

We would like to thank Stuart Atkinson for his invaluable
help in the preparation of this book.

Every effort has been made to contact copyright
holders of any material reproduced in this book. Any
omissions will be rectified in subsequent printings if
notice is given to the publisher.

Contents

Some words are shown in bold, **like this**. You can find them in the glossary on page 30.

Out of This World

There are many lights up in the night sky. These come from **stars**, **planets**, and other objects in space. If you look up at the sky on a clear night, you will be able to see hundreds of stars and some planets, too.

As our planet slowly turns, what we see in the night sky can change.

Large, bright comets with long tails can be seen about once every 10 years.

Comets only appear in our night sky from time to time. Comets can look like bright, hazy clouds with long tails or small, fuzzy gray balls.

5

Beliefs of the Past

In the past, people thought a comet meant bad luck. The ancient Chinese recorded comets. They also noted the disasters that they thought these comets caused.

This silk cloth records different comets seen in ancient China.

ISTI MIRANT STELLA

A comet that appeared in 1066 was included on this **tapestry** telling the story of William the Conqueror.

A bright comet appeared in 1066. People in England thought it was unlucky. Shortly after, England was invaded by a man called William the Conqueror and his army.

What Are Comets?

Comets are huge lumps of rock, dust, and ice, like huge, dirty snowballs. They are usually a few miles wide.

Comet Hale-Bopp shone brightly in the sky in 1997.

8

the Sun

comet

Comets are only close
to the Sun for part of
their journey.

Comets travel around the Sun. The Sun
is the center of our **solar system**. Comets
can be seen from Earth when they are
close to the Sun.

What Are Comets Made From?

The comets we see from Earth formed billions of years ago. Pieces of rock and ice clumped together to form the comet's **nucleus**. Comets may have a small **core** of solid rock.

The nucleus in the middle of a comet can be many different shapes.

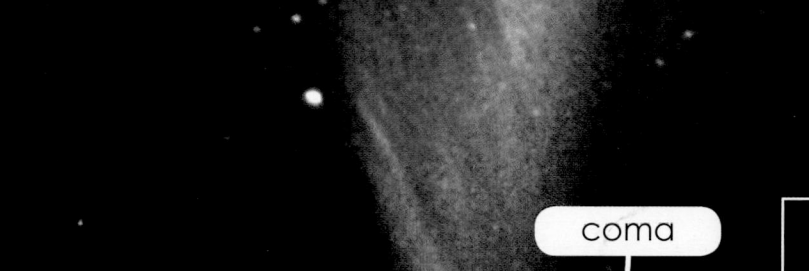

tail

coma

The nucleus of the comet is tiny when compared to the comet's tail.

When comets get close to the Sun, bits of ice and dust break off the comet. They form a hazy cloud called a **coma**. A tail of ice and dust streams out behind the comet.

Where Do Comets Come From?

Comets travel billions of miles across the **solar system**. Some comets travel from an area called the Kuiper Belt. It is on the edge of the solar system.

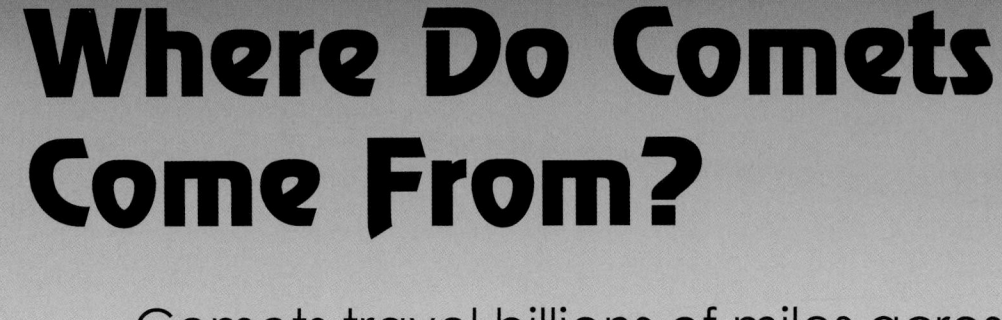

Some lumps of ice and rock in the Kuiper Belt are nearly as big as **planets**.

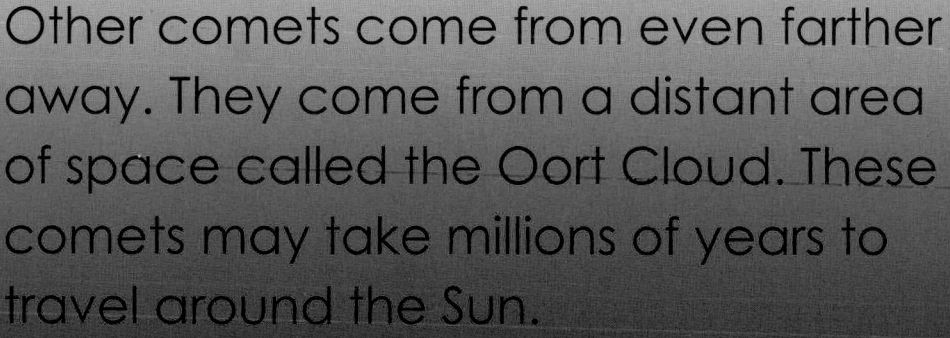

Some comets may have passed Earth only once since the time of the dinosaurs.

Other comets come from even farther away. They come from a distant area of space called the Oort Cloud. These comets may take millions of years to travel around the Sun.

Moving Close to the Sun

The comets we see in the night sky are moving very fast. A force called **gravity** makes them move around the Sun.

The comet Siding Spring passed by Earth in 2009.

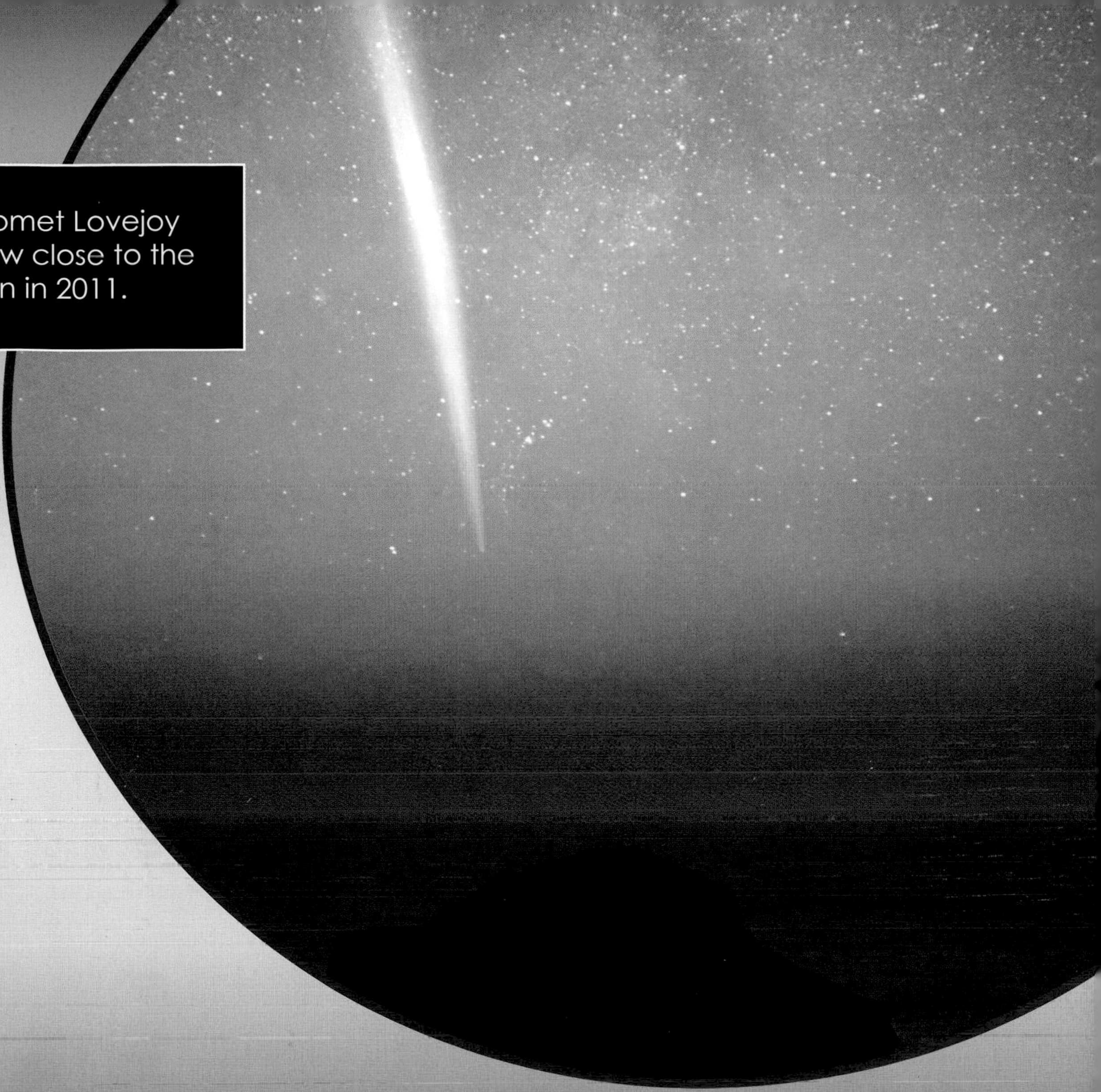

Comet Lovejoy flew close to the Sun in 2011.

Comets are heated by the Sun. By the time they can be seen from Earth, their tails can be millions of miles long. Sometimes comets crash into the Sun.

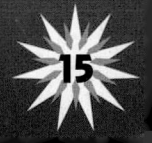

Halley's Comet

Halley's Comet is one of the most famous comets. It can be seen from Earth every 75 years. Halley's Comet last passed by Earth in 1986.

Halley's Comet is named after **astronomer** Edmond Halley.

Each year, Earth passes through a cloud of rocky pieces from Halley's Comet. They burn up when they hit Earth's **atmosphere**. We can see the light as they burn. We call this a **meteor shower**.

17

Comet Crashes

Comets' paths sometimes change. The force of **gravity** pulls them toward huge **planets**. The comet Shoemaker-Levy 9 crashed into the planet Jupiter in 1994.

The dark circle on this photograph shows where a piece of the Shoemaker-Levy 9 Comet hit Jupiter.

Water in Earth's oceans may have been brought here by comets.

Billions of years ago, many comets crashed into Earth. This happened long before people and animals existed. Another comet could crash into Earth sometime in the future.

Exploring Comets

Astronomers have been studying comets for thousands of years. Astronomers in ancient China were the first people to record comets. Today, comets can be studied with huge **telescopes**.

The Gemini telescope in Hawaii can observe comets that are far away in space.

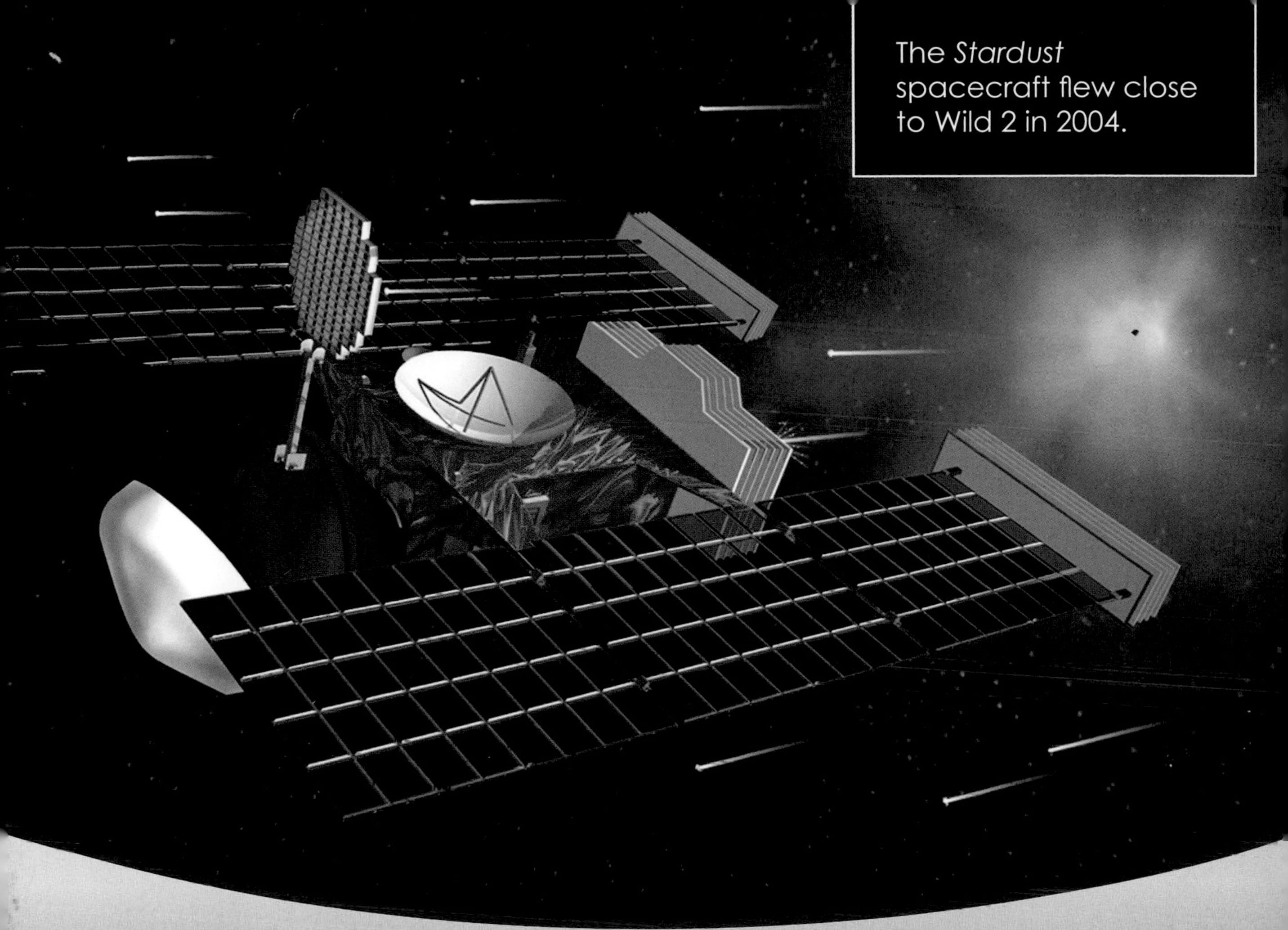

The *Stardust* spacecraft flew close to Wild 2 in 2004.

Astronomers can now use spacecraft to explore comets. The *Stardust* spacecraft collected samples of dust from the tail of a comet called Wild 2. This dust told us more about how comets formed.

Deep Impact

Deep Impact was the first spacecraft to tap into the **nucleus** of a comet. In 2005, it fired a piece of metal into the comet Tempel 1. Instruments on board sent back information about what came out of the nucleus.

The rocket carrying the *Deep Impact* spacecraft was launched from Florida in 2005.

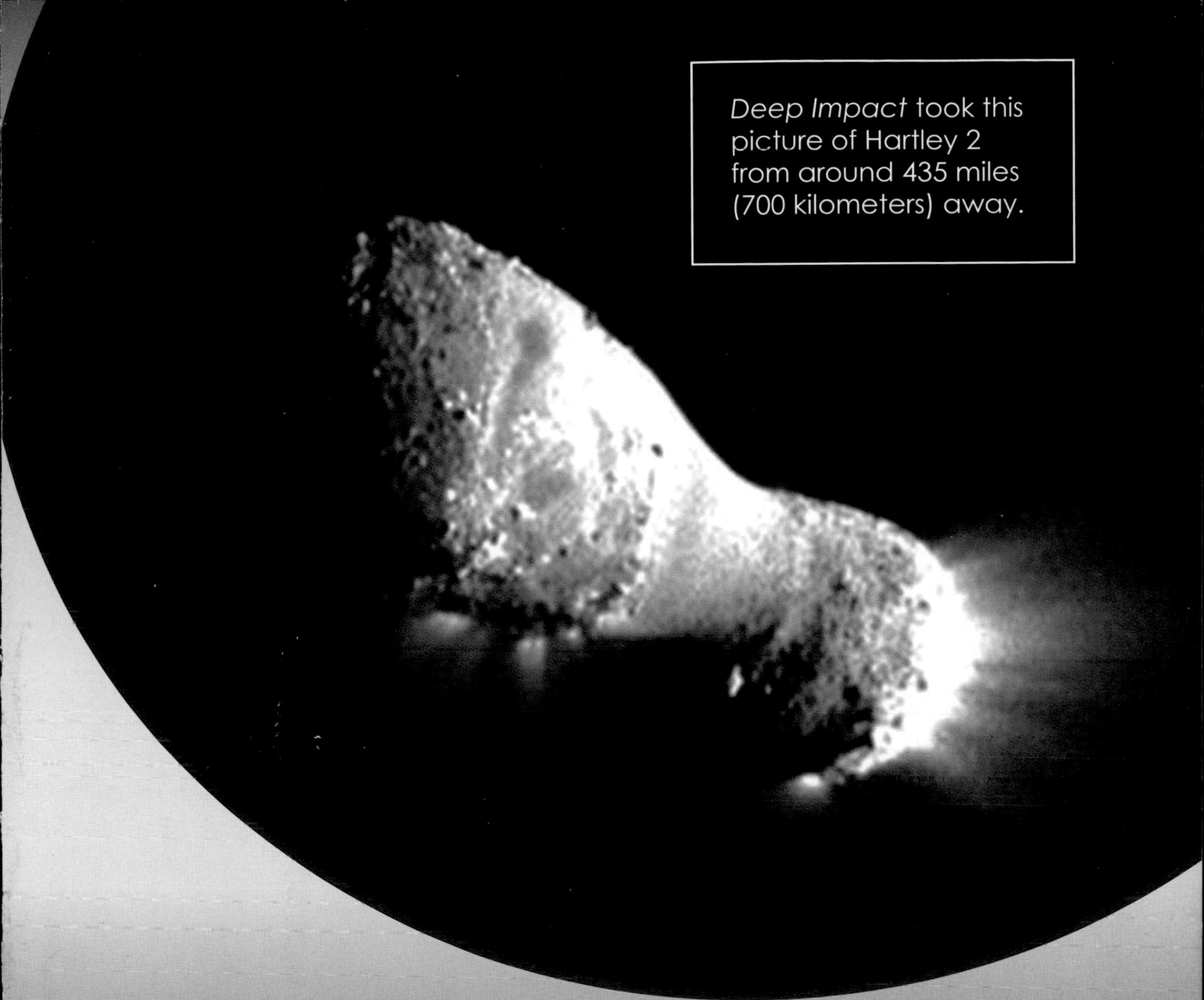

Deep Impact took this picture of Hartley 2 from around 435 miles (700 kilometers) away.

In 2011, *Deep Impact* passed close to a comet called Hartley 2. It took amazing close-up pictures of the comet. Jets of gas and dust were shooting out of the comet.

23

Discovering Comets

More than 800 comets have been discovered, but new comets are found every year. Most are so faint and far away that they can only be seen through a large **telescope**.

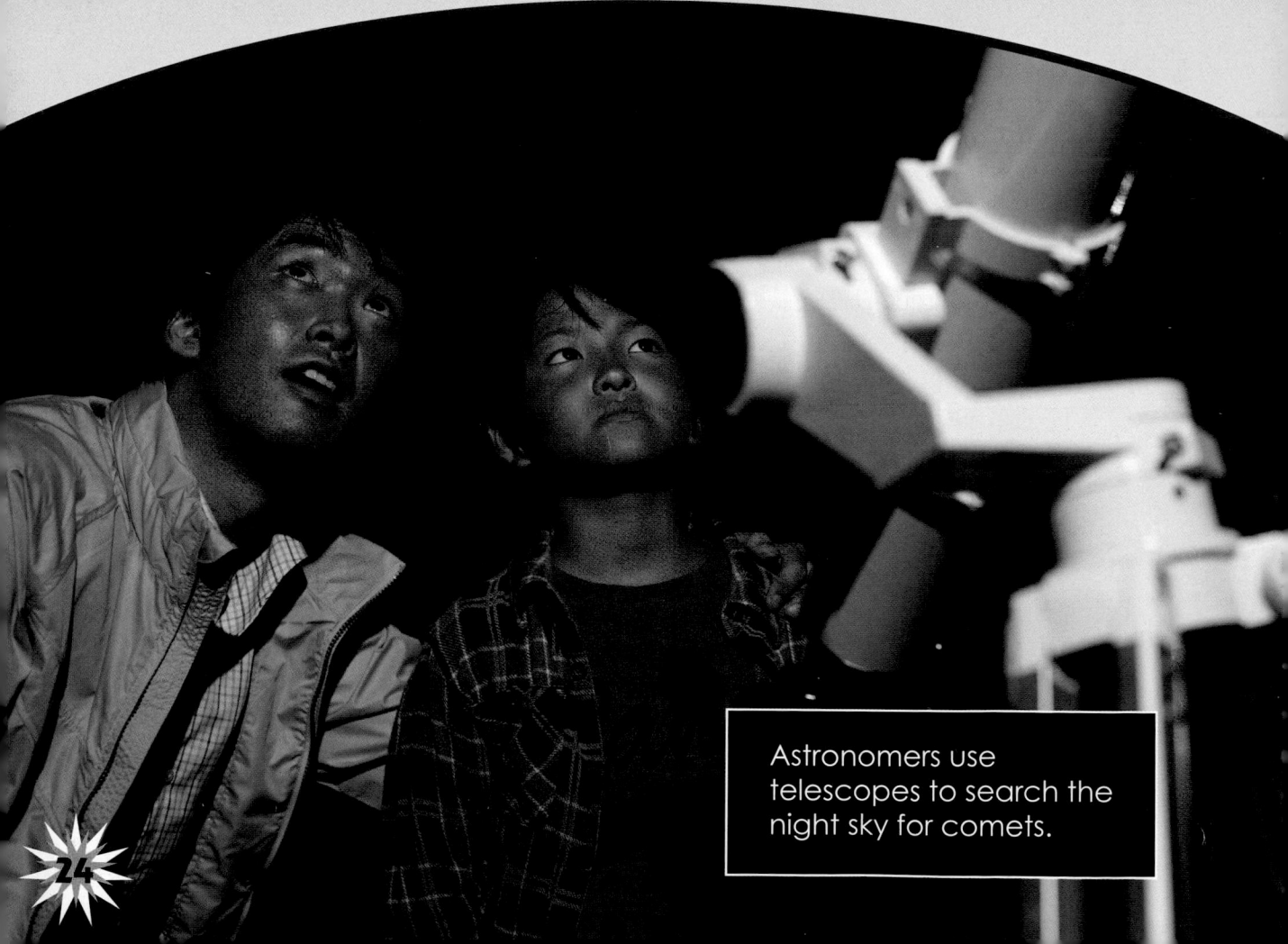

Astronomers use telescopes to search the night sky for comets.

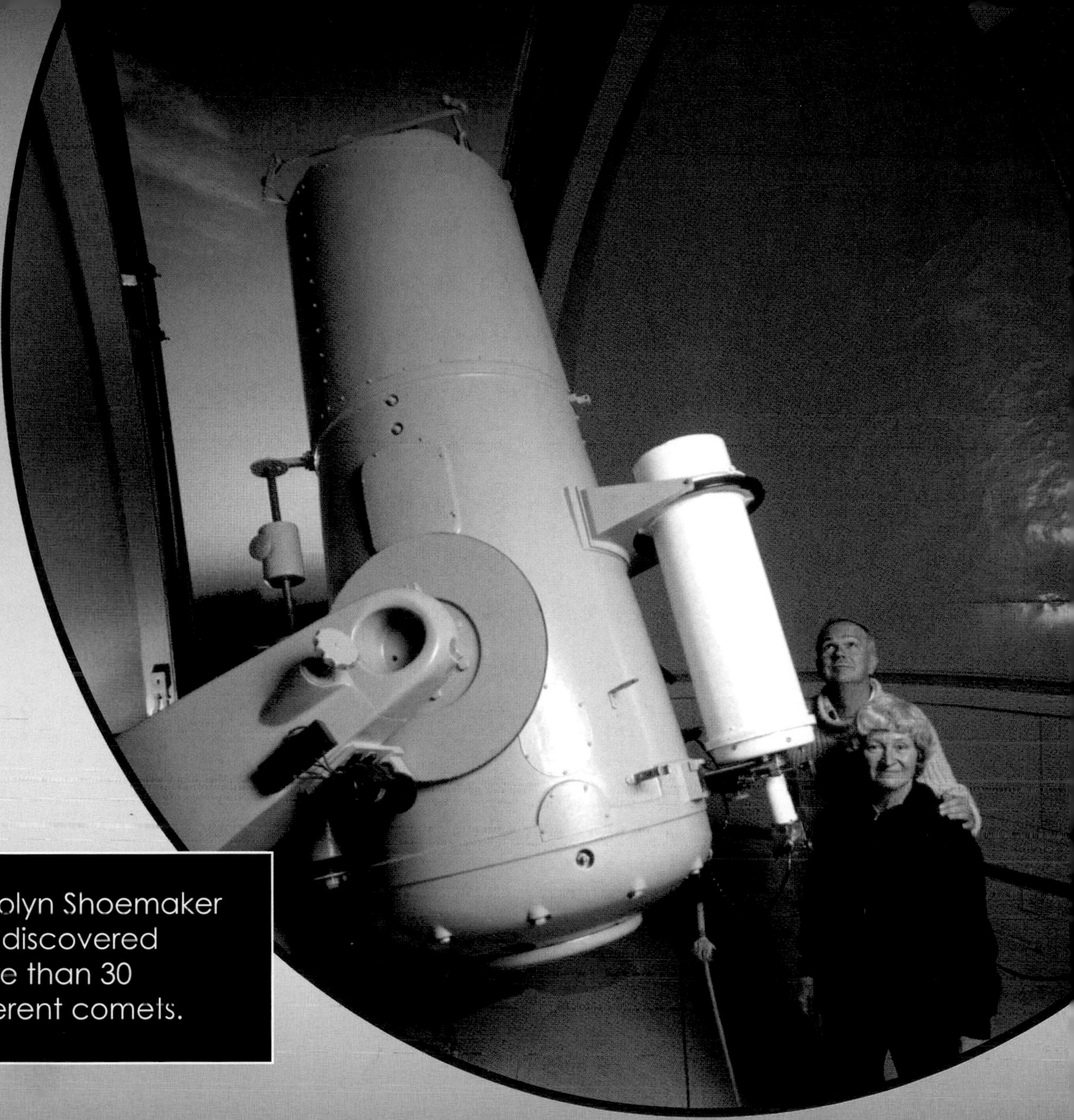

Carolyn Shoemaker has discovered more than 30 different comets.

Comets are usually named after the **astronomer** who found them. Some astronomers have discovered many comets.

See for Yourself

Halley's Comet will next pass Earth in 2061. Other comets will pass Earth before then. You can find out when comets are due to appear in the sky from space magazines and the Internet.

This comet was photographed in 2007. It was named McNaught, after the man who discovered it.

It is best to hunt for comets on a moonless night, when the sky is clear and dark.

You might even be able to find your own comet. **Astronomers** often find new comets crossing the sky. One day there could be a comet named after you!

Measuring Space

What you need:

- a ball
- a measuring wheel
- some friends to help measure distances
- lots of space.

Ask one friend to stand in the middle of a field, holding the ball.

If the ball is the Sun:

- Someone standing 2 yards (about 2 meters) from the ball would be Earth.
- The farthest **planet** from the Sun is Neptune, at 60 yards (about 55 meters) away.
- The Kuiper Belt, where some comets come from, would be around 109 yards (100 meters) away.
- The nearest part of the Oort Cloud would be about 6 miles (10 kilometers) away!

Glossary

astronomer person who studies space and the night sky

atmosphere layer of gases that surrounds a planet such as Earth

coma cloud of gas and dust around the nucleus of a comet

core middle of an object

gravity force that pulls all objects together and is usually only felt from large objects such as stars and planets

meteor shower lights in the sky caused by tiny pieces of rock from comets burning up in Earth's atmosphere

nucleus big lump of ice and rock at the center of a comet

planet large object (usually made of rock or gas) that orbits a star. Our planet, Earth, goes around the Sun.

solar system the Sun, eight planets, and many other small objects that travel around the Sun

star huge ball of burning gas that produces massive amounts of heat and light

tapestry cloth embroidered or decorated to make a picture with images sewn into it for decoration or to tell a story

telescope device that astronomers use to make things in space look bigger

Find Out More

Books

Bingham, Caroline. *First Space Encyclopedia*. New York: DK Children, 2008.

Kelley, J. A. *Meteor Showers* (True Books: Space). Danbury, Conn.: Children's Press, 2010.

Kortenkamp, Steve. *Asteroids, Comets, and Meteoroids* (Fact Finders: The Solar System and Beyond). Mankato, Minn.: Capstone, 2011.

Roza, Greg. *Comets and Asteroids: Space Rocks* (Our Solar System). New York: Gareth Stevens, 2010.

Web sites

Facthound offers a safe, fun way to find Internet sites related to this book. All of the sites on Facthound have been researched by our staff.

Here's all you do:

Visit **www.facthound.com**

Type in this code: 9781432975142

Index